Mangoes from the Seventh Dimension

Mangoes from the Seventh Dimension

1st Place
Winner of the
2022 Don Gutteridge Poetry Award

John Tyndall

Wet Ink Books

First Edition

Wet Ink Books
www.WetInkBooks.com
WetInkBooks@gmail.com

Title: Mangoes from the Seventh Dimension
Author: John Tyndall

Contest Judges: Don Gutteridge, John B. Lee
Cover Design: Richard M. Grove
Layout and Design: Richard M. Grove
Cover Image: Richard A. Kirk

Typeset in Garamond
Printed and bound in Canada
Distributed in USA by Ingram,
        — to set up an account — 1-800-937-0152

Library and Archives Canada Cataloguing in Publication

Title: Mangoes from the seventh dimension / John Tyndall.
Names: Tyndall, John, 1951- author.
Description: Poems. |
"1st place winner of the 2022 Don Gutteridge Poetry Award"
Identifiers: Canadiana 20230221866 |
        ISBN 9781989786840 (softcover)
Classification: LCC PS8589.Y5 M36 2023 |
        DDC C811/.54—dc23

Dedicated in memory to
my belovèd,
Diane Halpin

Contents:

– A Tom's Caution – *p. 1*

– Acids – *p. 3*

– Boogie Woogie Bugs Meet the Beetles – *p. 6*

– canada gees( ) – *p. 7*

– <click> – *p. 9*

– Cupbearer – *p. 10*

– Damned. – *p. 11*

– Danu – *p. 13*

– Dragonfreed – *p. 15*

– Editions of Kate / 2 4 6 8 10 9 7 5 3 1 – *p. 17*

– Even in Your Dreams – *p. 21*

– Fire Rede – *p. 22*

– Flinder's Fingers – *p. 23*

– Golden Joining, Golden Repair – *p. 24*

– Goosey – *p. 25*

– Installation – *p. 27*

– Is Everything Sacred? – *p. 29*

– It's a Sin – *p. 30*

– Johnny is a Bird Dog – *p. 31*

– Mangoes from the Seventh Dimension – *p. 33*

– Me grim – *p. 36*

– Mughal Miniature – *p. 37*

– *Neferkare Who Lives Forever* – *p. 39*

– Now on Sale – *p. 42*

– Off Two Decks – *p. 44*

– Pollen Angels – *p. 46*

– Pyramidion – *p. 47*

– PYROTHAN – *p. 48*

– *Quattro Pentimenti* – *p. 49*

– Revs – *p. 52*

– Secret Love – *p. 53*

– Silverpoint – *p. 54*

– SPECTACLES – *p. 55*

– *Sweetness and Light* versus *The Hairy Galoot* – *p. 56*

– *Tabulae Defixiones* – *p. 57*

– *The Beatles are Fire* – *p. 62*

– The King of Coif – *p. 64*

– The Pandora Books – *p. 66*

– The Second Time Alice Munro Asked Me a Question – *p. 69*

– Thou – *p. 71*

– Three Bird Hokku – *p. 72*

– To Keep Now Still – *p. 73*

– Tutankhamun's Mask – *p. 74*

– *Tysca*, Our Bird – *p. 75*

– Word Temple – *p. 76*

Acknowledgements – *p. 79*
Author Bio – *p. 81*

A Tom's Caution

Don't you ever dare call me
your sweet chocolate chip cat
I don't care what you dreamt
what a non-existent review
of a non-existent book
in a non-existent mag
said was your best line yet
because if I want a real poem
about a real son-of-a-mog
I'll head back overseas
to the land of poets I remember
from the red adventures
of all my sires before me
to hell with your *nine lives*
scads of dads in the past
we knew this author, Hugh
I think was his name
and although Esther, the poem's
woman was a fiction
that guy could really write
about torn ears, sharp teeth
the fights and the screams
so I don't give a flying finch
about all the exotic timcats
who loll about you all day
and you'd better believe
I could sail to Blighty
aboard any ship I choose
and when I got there
I wouldn't languish
on a gravesite like some dog
I'd be catching and killing
hot and kicking rabbits
because while you apes

were struggling to quit
the homey, leafy canopy
my ancestors were kings
of the desert night
and surviving on blood
without a drop of water
thus, my precious monkey
take heed, for if you ever
call *me* your chocolate chip cat
I'll scratch your eyes out

Acids

Window Pane

The last time he took
lysergic acid diethylamide-25
he got off at the beach
in the water, in the sunshine
and the flotation was
as they say, groovy
and back at the cottage
while he was stoned
the hamburgers tasted like cardboard
and the whole trip
lasted too long, as usual
but Jimi's "Moon, Turn the Tides"
flew outside and mingled
with the shouts of playing children
then a brown thrasher sang duet
with John McLaughlin's guitar
on the opening of "Birds of Fire"
and nobody freaked out
least of all him

Blotter

He took LSD on March 5, 1971
with a Peace Frog on it
and while at the bus stop
the ground heaved and undulated
the bus he rode downtown
disappeared and he soared along
avenues, swung around curves
like a planet around the sun
and oh cliché, oh wow
he ended up mesmerized
by a black-light poster
at the combination head shop
and record dealer
but the greatest miracle
on this strange day, he never
splattered dirt on himself
during his journey through
snow-melt muddy streets
and at the peak of it all
he rhymed off album titles
in chronological order
not even forgetting *The Beatles' Story*
before *Beatles '65* before *Beatles VI*
and he returned from chaos
with only a few bits of his self
lost forever

Orange Barrel

The first time he took acid
it was high school graduation
he'd skipped the ceremony
got bored by the party
swallowed the 500 mics
and ended up out west
in a nighttime suburb
hearing all of The Doors'
Morrison Hotel in a flash
while the song "Mississippi Queen"
steamed along for hours
and, hey man, the stars
spoke to him in tongues
shag carpeting grew mushrooms
and he looked like an electric ghost
when he got home again
and went to bed too soon
his brain spewed rapid pictures
the most transcendent one being
Mickey Mouse using his feet
on a gigantic fretboard
to play "Whole Lotta Love"
and the last things he saw
just before he fell asleep
were raindrops trailing off
on a forest pond
thus the only beautiful
experience was the drug
leaving his bloodstream
and as for the rest, well
it was all M-I-C-

Boogie Woogie Bugs
Meet the Beetles

Almost
strains of Guy Lombardo
through the beech saplings
along the south riverbank
when you spy something
something pale on a black branch
is it moss or lichen or fungus
zoom in and see for yourself
thousands of white filaments
and then in extreme close-up
the blight comes alive
as aphids shake their booty
like Busby Berkeley babes
they dance to an ancient beat
that dazzles most predators
but when you pan the narrow stage
almost Wonderland Gardens in miniature
you focus on hungry beetles
from way across the pond
all of them shaped
like pudding-bowl haircuts
and you swear you can
hear one shout *Hey, guys*
I've got a toppermost idea.
Why don't we perform
right here, right now.

One, two, three, fah!

canada gees( )

For bill bissett

Hey, bill
the Canada geese
are throat-singing
again, mate
to mate
their heads bob
bowing in bonded
recognition
and woe betide
the unlucky primate
interposing itself
between this pair

Danger : Gander

Yes, and now
two Canada geese
are in distress
at a metal fence
a downy gosling
on the wrong side
from mother goose
cannot return
the way it entered
under chain-links
and needs the aid
of a buff athlete
to reach home

My miracle
escape, Ma

No sign, bill
of hummingbirds
hitchhiking
with this flock
but there happened
a wondrous flight
beleev it or not
of a bumblebee
over patio stones
whose wing-beats
stirred up tiny
dust clouds

helicopter
miniature

\<click\>

In this digital age
microwave transmitters
and fibre-optic cables
bring voices both real
and simulacrum to you
pinpoint your location
for hucksters local
and global (think
Kitchener, think
Karachi) voices
clear and close
as devils or angels
in your head, notice
the hubbubbling background
operator upon operator
speaking at different places
in the same spiel, notice
the pause
before some hard seller
congratulates your luck
winning a virtual contest
the telephone rings
again you hope
for a belovèd
or a friend
you answer *Hello*
the message corrects
'Hello' is an invalid
response, press 1
now

Cupbearer

Twenty-three centuries
after Alexander the Great
stabled his dark war-
stallion Bucephalus
long enough to marry
royal Achaemenid women
to Macedonian men
mingling the Eastern
and the Western, body
to body, his cupbearer
of the golden rhyton
mixing wine and water
for the wedded guests
twenty-three centuries later
our server at Mykonos
Restaurant brings
our retsina, our ouzo
and while he asks us all
to call him Gary, his name
is no diminutive of Garvey
Germanic for *spear-bearer*
but of Garshasb, Persian for
rider of the black horse
an ancient nomen his mother
read in a volume of poems
in the Persic tongue and, lo
our regal cupbearer
how we shall sing his story

Damned.

I woke from a dream
to the pitch and yaw
of my ship sailing
out from Africa
ahead of a storm
bound for the Indies
with shackled cargo
yes, I dreamt a dream
brief but unholy
I gazed in a glass
obsidian black
looted from Aztecs
and my bearded face
changed before my eyes
all of it shining
like carved emeralds
slave-mined and stolen
from Colombia
and it spoke to me
I am the green one
then it disappeared
and I woke to thirst
and hunger and lust

I do what I will
in my own cabin
whomever I choose
but I'm filled with fear
of plagues and of fire
I'm haunted by each
moaning singing voice
I have bought and sold

I hate their darkness
the depths of their souls
my skin now so pale
I avoid the day
so wan my body
burns and burns and burns
even under all
the stars of Goshen

Danu

I come to her river
on a spring morning
mist rising, robin returning
when I hear the splash
of her horse's hoofs
'tis Danu, queen
of the Celtic gods
of the green isle
she bends to caress
my cheek, saying
Come here
I thee encharm
and when she departs
an elflock, twisted
in my beard, remains

I come to her river
at midsummer noon
cloud floating, finch circling
in the blue heavens
and from atop her steed
Danu, the mother of all
leans to caress my cheek
my head, saying
Come here
I thee encharm
Come to me
I thee enchant
and when she rides off
elflocks, twisted in my beard
in my hair, remain

I come to her river
on an autumn evening
rain falling, blackbird leaving
Danu, the great goddess
dismounts at the river-bank

stretches to caress my cheek
my head, my spine, saying
Come here
I thee encharm
Come to me
I thee enchant
Come at my call
I thee ensorcell
and when she remounts
and disappears upriver
elflocks, twisted in my beard
in my hair, down my back, remain

I come to her river
at midnight mid-winter
ice cracking, crow sleeping
under the silver stars
Danu, mistress of changes
strides towards me
reaches to caress my cheek
my head, my spine
my waist, saying
Come here
I thee encharm
Come to me
I thee enchant
Come at my call
I thee ensorcell
Come with me now away
I thee enthrall
and when she claims
her stallion charger
elflocks, twisted in my muzzle
my forelock, my mane
my tail, remain
forevermore

Dragonfreed

You rescue a dragonfly
helpless, half-drowned
from a rain-puddle
carefully place the insect
on a wooden railing
where it will surely
recover and zoom away

You return awhile later
the dragon sits motionless
its wingtips adhered
to the painted surface
so you release those
delicate transparencies
with a tamarack twig
now it will most surely
recover and zoom away

You return after a moment
and this Canada Darner clings
by five legs in the summer wind
and cannot ride the gusts
wingtips stuck together
on both sides of its body
again you wield the little stem
and the four freed wings
certainly mean the creature will
recover and zoom away

You return almost immediately
and *Aeshna canadensis*
still hasn't flown aloft
one leg tethered to one eye
by a filament of spider-web

requires your skilful touch
with a birch-wood toothpick
and now the leg is free
the eye-bulb is free
the wings free
in an instant
buzz and zoom away

Editions of Kate / 2 4 6 8 10 9 7 5 3 1

But Kate Bush is the only angel left.
Lee 'Scratch' Perry

2   '78

Wow, she heralds
winged lioness
rampant gold blazon
looking for perpetual
Peter Pan from Baghdad
to Kensington, looking
for lovers Emma
and Kashka

4   '82

Harry escapes
heaven's chains
journeys onwards
to gardens in Gaffa
the outback of Woomera
he pulls the pin
and blows the safe
for a rain of tenners
Kate's kiss
the key

6   '89

Secrets of anger
and love so deep
you cannot confide
in other angels
cannot confess
to divinity
asking permission
for Yes

No
only Bulgarka choirs
and birth cries
reach you

8   '05

Saint Elvis Aaron eats
and recites 3.14159
atop a mountain of snow
the angel of laundry
is invisible
and Jeanne d'Arc prays
with the coral queen
kneeling on fleurs-de-lis
as Ariel the Painter
surrounded by doves
colours the sunset
the sunrise
honey
song of blackbird
shush of waves
angels laugh
at daybreak

10   '11

A snow angel
makes love
with a snowman
snowflakes find the wild
Himalayan man
and Catherine
is being born anew
waiting for icy windows
to open, waiting
to find me again

9 '11

She's got to dream
to laugh
the kissing bite you need
on your angel's shoulder
asking permission
for Yes again
Yes
Molly and Raphael
Sharon and Marion
Lily and Gabriel
Michael and Uriel
love on fire in love

7 '93

A clockwork diva
run by rubber bands
dances for Solomon
in scarlet ballet slippers
as he pulls off
his old boots, woollen socks
she eats his song, says
Why should an angel
love you

5 '85

That cloud
could wake a witch
that whirlybird sound
could kill the hound
a-hunting, Kate
skate over me
frozen in mid-stream
my watch-face still

glows in darkness
come run up my spine
like God would
if she could

3   '80

Babooshka
swathed in headscarf
kisses a little boy
breathes in his elemental
poisons, only later
releases them
from beneath her
swirling skirts
all to a lost chorus
of Delius'
violins

1   '78

Sun and moon
surprised by a kite
string clutched
in a stranger's hands
his childlike eyes
haunted by them
heavy spirits
at Wuthering Heights
and Scratch
is sadly dancing
for Cathy, angelic
ghost in tears
tapping
the pane, the pain

Even in Your Dreams

Up from your unconscious
come the unusual characters
for tonight's show, starting
with long-dead songster Tim Buckley
of bohemian nimbus hair
who rails against one
staid television network
replacing his performances
"Hallucinations" and "Dream Letter"
with the Ray Conniff Singers
clean-coiffed and crew cut
crooning "Somewhere My Love"
before he morphs into your
aunt, the one dying
in a backwater hospital
but here she's young, blonde
able to shout about her
first husband's demand
she entertain his cousins
at a lakeside barbeque
with too little practice
and then you're eating
in a swank bistro
she's now the waitress
under a retro Afro
taking your seafood order
while she yearns to serve
only one loving partner
you behold an arcing halo
like photographic flare
over her bright face
and when you wake
in bedroom darkness
your familiar migraine aura
those twinkling lights, persists
so you'd better suck on
the *zolmitriptan* quickly before
your nightmare really begins

Fire Rede

I have looked
into flames
seen and unseen
many scenes
set fires
fed fires
felt warmth
felt burns
and never
go they out
and never
eat they me
not fuel
but free
I gaze
with fire
and rise

Flinders' Fingers

Flinders Petrie
on Egyptian expedition
methodically dug
down through layers
of potsherds, layers
of remote time
detailed the fragments
recorded their location
devised a classification
of successive cultures
and even where no
vessels remained *in situ*
sometimes the contents
somehow still lingered
with sand much darker
at one ancient level
where his fingers
the first in millennia
and in the name of Her
Majesty, Queen Victoria
grasped and released
fragrant sacred perfume
for the Scorpion god

Golden Joining, Golden Repair

When I came bro
-ken you mended me
with gold-of-heart dust
and the lacquer of love
I, rough *Raku* ware
shaped by hands
a generation ago
bore heavily my age
showed covertly my wear
so you taught the way
the ceremony of tea
in a special room
painted goddess green
bringing the liquid
to a slow simmer
wiping me clean
with warm cloth
and I in my turn
whisked you to froth
as we learned the path
of quiet acceptance
of transience
of imperfection
for, together
through simplicity
with asymmetry
we have found
beauty and serenity

Goosey

Flotilla all in a line
moves against river-flow
like fighting frigates
commanded by Nelson
or Jack Aubrey
straight at the foe
a rival fleet of geese
and the two captains
shoot volleys of beaks
and wind-beating wings
until the enemy scatters
with its defeated gander
every one of them honks
in tones of despair
while the victors sound
their cries of triumph

*

Further upstream
another line of geese
rides the current
approaching rapids
and while some steer
to backwater eddies
and others take wing
to calmer waters
an adventurous core
traverses the curling course
extreme thrill-seekers
exhilarated, arriving
for the next challenge

*

However, some of us
Branta canadensis
prefer the riverbank
preening and feeding
and observing
the goosey behaviour
of passing primates

Installation

For M-J Idzerda

On a riverbank path
hurrying north upstream
for a movie matinée
I passed a cut stone seat
usually for resting alumni
taking in the campus view
but on that stone someone
had placed three *objets d'art*
which looked at first sight
to be women's fashion sunglasses
a switchblade and a DVD
digital, encoded side up

and my imagination leapt
at the story the trio told
how you play the video to
discover if she was a victim
or a *femme fatale* with a flick-
knife starring in a neo-*noir* flick
maybe you have to juggle
the shiny things, try to catch
and toss them high in the air
making sure to grasp the dagger
by its mother-of-pearl handle
put on and take off the shades
while mind-reading the disc, hey
somebody in the props department
must have had the urge
to mount an installation
wide-open gallery
free admittance

On the way home downstream
with more time to devote
to the work on display
I realized I'd had it all wrong
the sunglasses were men's aviator
the knife, a fishing lure
and the DVD, a CD
digital, encoded side down
its label said *Gold*
by Cher, Disc One

altogether
another tale

Is Everything Sacred?

If everything is sacred
you vibrate in ec-
stasis
afraid to offend
anxious about each
matter on your path
you, passionate in the face
of myriad gods, this rock
that tree, those birds
divinities demanding
perpetual prayer
even reflections upon still
waters only you can see
holy
even the mites alive
on your body
consecrated
even the fragrance
of your asparagus piss
blessèd
or
you, amazed
before the angry God
who hallows times
and spaces, speaking
particles and waves
and the bonds that bind
with but one voice
if everything is sacred
you quiver for all life
and *then* you fucking
die

It's a Sin

With apologies to Harper Lee

We've all seen them
been passed unnoticed
by plugged-in people
walking or jogging or cycling
their earphones replacing
the sound of journeys
with news of war
hip-hop hits
books in bytes
how they ignore wind
and water signs
but worst of all to me
how they block out
songbird song-bursts
the Oriole, the Cardinal
sweetly throated thrushes
or tiny warblers
of grand voices

Listen
surely you can hear
that cool jazzer
from a beatnik café
that northern cousin
of Mr. Mocker

Shut out all
the Blue Jays you want
if you can avoid them
but remember
it's a sin
to miss a Catbird

Johnny is a Bird Dog

He must be crazy, his eyes
tracking the flight downriver
of a Belted Kingfisher
even more brilliant blue
than his Ron Milton miniature
his voice whispering
Made my day
while he's missed a flirty
ponytail swishing by
on a beautiful jogger
but he's been like this forever
his Akela shouting
from two-toned '56 Chevy
Hey, bird dog
because he was always
looking, looking up
and the swallows
leave *la misión de*
San Juan Capistrano
on his birthday, yes
sometimes he's so excited
watching Hooded Mergansers
those harlequins, dive
between ice-floes
watching Cedar Waxwings
pass through on their way
north in the springtime
south in the autumn
watching Black-Capped Chickadees
ransack every branch
of an insect-laden tree
that he even thinks
he's a bird

As the Kingfisher vanishes
far away in morning shadow
Johnny's gaze rises above the water
to behold an eagle
a Bald Eagle
white head
brown body
white tail
the whole *águila*
and he's about to whisper
when a second
mature
adult
following its mate
looking down, thinks
He's a dog

Mangoes
from the Seventh Dimension

They say that time
the greatest animator
this side of Walt's
passing particles
can somehow present
a seventh dimension
but who are *they* anyway
and could they view
cartoons of dancing mangoes
with 7D glasses

You scientists
can you predict
the propagation
of right-handed neutrinos
in a seventh
warped dimension
and can you trace
their pattern of decay
not unlike the cross-
sectioned curves
of ripe mango

We may experience
difficulty monitoring
interactions
in the seventh
dimension, so
accustomed are we
to supermarket
transactions
for imported mangoes
with folding money

or flat cards multiplying
the height of folly
by the length of credit
with no discernible
depth of feeling

She loves to eat
faraway fresh mangoes
peeling plumpness
slathering hands
lips, chin
with juices so pungent
she never wears
perfume

He prefers to drink
out-of-this-world
mango *lassis*
sweetie syrup
milky sway
salty crystals
chilled, chilled
to slake all
his thirsts

You, dear reader
ignore rumours
out of the Philippines
at your peril
dare dismiss
portals reported
in island jungles
sightings of child-
like beings offering

strange baskets
of succulent mangoes
from the seventh
dimension

I and I
alone have discovered
proof of this fruit
from afar yet closer
than a kiss, at once
there
at the string-end
of space/time and
here
in this garbage can
an empty plastic wrapper
7D Dried Mangoes

Me grim

The weke and feble eyes of the world, deseased
with the mygrim and accustomed to darcknesse.
William Tyndale

O fie
pain returns to my skull
again and again harbingers
flash before my eyes
a new moon of gems)
or sword slash of fire /
they veil you, my belovèd
hide the pages on my desk
mask the groundlings in the pit

Would that all light
be shrouded like a red lamp
all noise hushed
like a slow stream

The megrim strikes upon the right
one day and next day
upon the left, a game
of shuttlecocks at court

O begone
that I might pick up
my quill, my brushes
and live and create
not be hung at the crossroads
nor beheaded in the Tower

but a cool cloth upon my brow
your kiss upon my lips
and away from the dark
I will arise to write, to play on

Mughal Miniature

With thanks to Donovan

A gift from my belovèd
in our flower garden
a book of Mughal miniatures
opens at the plate
lovers in a blue pavilion
with musical instruments
exotic fruit and birds
alas, only a reproduction

*

ah, now the painting itself
upon a gallery wall
and the ornamental tent
is lapis lazuli blue
the man and the woman
gaze eye to eye
their sitar and tamboura
recently set aside
plums and pomegranates at hand
peafowl under the trees
I stare longingly
long enough
until

*

I am hiding like a child
on a carved balcony
watching the royal pair
their canopy scented
with sandalwood
in my mind's ear
I still hear their music
their morning raga
of love and surrender

a silver salver holds
plums and pomegranates
mangoes and tangerines
the peacock shakes
one thousand and one
iridescent eyes
before the shy peahen
but wait
the bearded prince
his face
is

                    *

mine
alone with her
in sunshine glints
upon pearls
and diamonds
star rubies
star sapphires
we pull open
our saffron silks
and crimson brocades
she lets fall
her soft, dark tresses
over turquoise earrings
I part her hair with a sigh

bestow kisses
upon her lips

enter her garden

Neferkare Who Lives Forever

Horus name
Horus Netjerikhaw
Horus, Divine of Apparition

who outlives mother Ankhesenmeryre II
she hears the book of the dead
she sees the pyramid texts

not have I spoken lies
not have I committed offence
not have I caused grief
not have I harmed
not have I done evil

mother of alabaster
translucent skin
the little king
in her lap

Nebti name
Nebti Netjerikhaw
The Two Ladies, Divine of Apparition

who outlives sister-wife Iput II
who outlives half-sister-wife Neith
they hear the book of the dead
they see the pyramid texts

not have I despoiled the things of the god whose two eyes are of fire
not have I afflicted any of flame
not have I transgressed blazing legs from the darkness
not have I inflamed myself with rage of speech
not have I carried away offerings from the beautiful ones

belovèd king's wives
tiny pyramids

buried boats
borrowed sarcophagi

Horus of Gold name
Sekhem Bik-Nebu
The Golden Falcon is Powerful

who outlives general Sasenet
he hears the book of the dead

not have I committed fornication
not have I been an eavesdropper
not have I defiled the wife of a man doubly wicked
not have I defiled the wife of a man from the torture chamber
not have I polluted myself looker at what is brought

alone with his king
four hours of the night
within his chambers
and upon his bed
four hours of the night

Throne name
Neferkare
Beautiful is the Soul of Re

who outlives son Ptahshepses
he hears the book of the dead
he sees the pyramid texts

not have I carried off bones
not have I desolated plowed lands
not have I made curses of seasons
not have I defrauded the offerings of the gods
not have I slaughtered the cattle divine

the prince of Dakhla region
lord of oases
lord of caravans
coming forth from Nubia
he wears a golden belt
from the mines of Nubia

**Birth name
Sa Re Pepi II
Son of Re Pepi II**

who outlives servant Harkhuf
he hears the book of the dead

*not have I slain men of shades
not have I eaten my heart from the secret place
not have I caused terror of the mighty
not have I judged hastily of faces
not have I carried off the food of the infant*

he bears a gift
for his child king Pepi II
more beautiful than ivory
more wondrous than gold
he inspects the gift
ten times at night
he appoints worthy men
to guard the gift
his majesty desires to possess
from the land of horizon dwellers

a pygmy
a pygmy of the god's dances

Now on Sale

Hey Marty says Roger
from the back seat
There's a huge sale
on now and he's right
the Ford dealership
here in depressed Windsor
shouts it in desperation
yellow and black signs
one after another
        HUGE
        SALE
         ON
        NOW
          !
And to a car brimming
with coffee-fueled poets
this is an event

Hey Roger I say
from the other
side of Susan
Now is on sale
and I wonder
who's going to wear
that ultimate plaid jacket
and be awarded
the top trophy
for moving the most
new models
        HUGE
        SALE
         ON
        NOW
          !

Everything has a price
that no-one can afford
the water squeezed along
the Detroit River
bought and sold
the air tainted
by burn-offs
speculated about
and pegged to some
money-making algorithm
    HUGE
    SALE
     ON
    NOW
     !

Someone wants to sell you
every moment you experience
every kiss you kiss
every love you love
so climb into the back seat
with your favourite poets
and get a little piece of the action
    NOW
     IS
     ON
    SALE
     !

And it's huge

Off Two Decks

'Twas only last month
upon a shaded deck
with a sunny view
of Long Point Bay
in Norfolk County
that a flock of poets
sang and read aloud
in good fellowship
when Sergeant Jack Russell
the growling guardian
went on a walkabout
with his mistress
allowing an emboldened
Northern Flicker
to alight on the lawn
to delve in the soil
its beak tossing aside
worker ants in favour
of flavorous larvae
like a writer searching
through a word hoard
for *le mot juste*
to perfect the poem

'Twas many months ago
upon this very deck
near the John Wise Line
in Elgin County
the poets congregated
with fresh stanzas
spoken to hungry ears
when Mister Henry Tiger
the roving feline
returned to his home
with a rabbit still
kicking in his jaws
retired beneath nearby spruce
to rend, to tear, to devour
his leporine lunch
oblivious to all
the bloodless arts

Pollen Angels

If she could escape, she thought, just for a moment, out
of her personal mind into their communally single one, she
would know at last what it was like to be an angel.

David Malouf, *Remembering Babylon*

Out of hexagonal cells
sexless sisters fly forth
to ensure the ripened
fruit of the tree
which is in the midst
of the garden, yea
even of the tree of life

Without these squadrons
of soldiering workers
you would look unto a land
flowing with neither
milk nor honey

To you, mirror image
of the Hiver of heaven
flights of pollen angels
wing their way, how many
may dance upon you

Be not afraid
of their sacred sound
their flaming sword
east of the sunrise

Be still

Let them swarm

Pyramidion

I.M. Cynthia Norris

While I was reading *The Egyptian Necklace*
or looking in my bowl for cereal bits that formed
the sun disk carried by the boat of the moon
or building pylons and hypostyle halls with toy blocks
Cynthia was climbing the Great Pyramid of Giza
all the way to the dizzying top with a local guide
a guide who clutched *her* arm in fear all the way down
her ascent and descent the culmination of a journey
through Africa with her parents and her older sister
a journey akin to *The Poisonwood Bible* although no-one
died from the bite of the Black Mamba or the Sacred Cobra
and when she came home she brought with her artful mysteries
turning her apartments and homes into temples of Bastet
graced by her felines Sada then Simone then Iris
creating with never-idle hands quilt after quilt after quilt
and it was my good fortune to receive as a gift one
entitled *Sticks and Stones* in a version deconstructing
the original pattern with every block and every stitch
forming triangles and steps like all the pyramids of the Nile
when I look closely I see Cynthia going forth from the east bank
in the Black Land west to the plateau in the Red Land
soaring as though a feather outweigh her heart and soul
bringing with her the white limestone casing blocks
to cover the dark limestone core of ancient Khufu's Horizon
how she rises to the apex gazing to the lapis lazuli
skies of evening with the setting sun reflecting upon
her perfected self the very electrum-gilded pyramidion

PYROTHAN

For Ray Hsu, four voices

I must drive my car   I walk every day
now I have to bike   *you can change yourself*

haven't you a bell   **don't you cut me off**

spaces you may share   ***get off the roadway***

walk on the right side   *temper your demands*

don't step out in front   use your damn signal

your eyes be open   ***do you never look***
why can't you see me   **are you always blind**

burn you up alive   send you to the sun
set your car afire   *please, please, O please, please*

Quattro Pentimenti

A new exhibit
on the uppermost floor
of the renovated gallery
collects and displays
examples of pentimento
in the paintings
of Caravaggio, Titian
and Pieter de Hooch
come hear volunteer
Kristen's talk
she will elucidate
the difference
between artists who
changed their minds
and artists whose
figures overlaid
completed backgrounds
she will demonstrate
how to discover evidence
by looking aslant
as a ray of light

*

The four McKay brothers
moved in on Owen Sound
across from a rival store
in the year of our Lord 1905
and by 1924 for the sum
of sixty thousand dollars
bought them out lock and stock
and you can still discern
that moment in history
advertised on the building
at 942 Second Avenue East
once named Poulett Street
where McKAY'S DRY GOODS
cannot hide the older RYAN BROS
even after all these years

                    *

Curse or bless
those student painters
working with White Album
white semi-gloss latex
who rolled a living-room wall
with the words Helter Skelter
then covered them with coat
after coat after coat
so you could still see
the snappy song title
leering out at you
at odd moments
in bright day
or incandescent night

                    *

Time the rogue packs
width to waists, grays
auburn or bronze hair
adds lines and saggings
to faces and limbs
of two ageing lovers
but memory sees youth
even as far back as
adolescent journeys to
the Venice glass-works
on *Isola di Murano*
and the Italian pavilion
for Expo 67
on *Île Notre-Dame*
behind and before
their very eyes
where there is no
change of heart

Revs

So I find myself
lost in suburban acres
roads laid out off
any grid in planning
ranch house after ranch house
no sidewalks, no gutters
no streetlights, no illumination
everything unfinished
lost, but here comes the light
from a 1966 Mini Cooper
and George Harrison rolls
down his driver's window
says, *Care for a lift, sailor?*
and I climb right in
settle back in black leather
telling him I dreamed of
Sgt. Pepper's Lonely Hearts Club Band
a dream I dreamed weeks before its release

So I find myself
in Mary's Record Mart
discovering in The Beatles' bin
the long-awaited album
looking on the back cover, all
one bright, solid colour
to see if it includes the songs
Strawberry Fields Forever
and Penny Lane, *searching*
through columns and columns
of words and more words
but nowhere can I locate them

George smiles and smiles and smiles
revs his magical Tantric motor
and drives me out of suburbia
so I find myself

Secret Love

This floral affair
began innocently
when he thought to
shower with their
Phalaenopsis orchid
instead of misting
its leaves, its flowers

Gradually nearer
and nearer soft
pink petals swayed
but a lick away
from wet skin
green-tipped roots
quested for attention

Soon his night-dreams
blushed so much
with moth orchids
and his daydreams
with butterfly blooms
he worried, feared
his human partner
might discover
his inter-species love
and perform a bilateral
orchidectomy
with garden shears

Silly boy, every day
in the same room
she's made furry tryst
with their purring cat
whispering in a loving tongue
El gato naranja
El gato rojo

Silverpoint

For Richard A. Kirk

On a grounding
pristine as snowfall
each fine line drawn
with silver wire
you can never erase
from prepared paper
fur of vixen
feathers of raven
appeared under the stylus
of renaissance artist
but now outstretched
arms of women end
in birch branches
and the uncrowned
king of tattered flocks
ponders rhinoceros beetle
every curve and arabesque
so surreal, so perfectly
argentine, line by line
you pluck from desire
shaded bird bones
sternum, wing and skull
grinding them down
for a grounding

S
PE
CTA
CLES

The trail I take
along the riverside
has become The Way
looking through my new
crystal spectacles
even flies are in focus
as they flee aeronautic
and acrobatic swallows
shining feathered visions
able to veer and spin
climb and dive
every hungry lunge
each sip on the wing
clear to my sights
and further upstream
blue brilliant flash
as kingfisher plunges
disappears, splash appears
clutching a silver fish
it flaps to farther shore
where I can make out
the wriggling tail-fin
going down and gone

Sweetness and Light
versus *The Hairy Galoot*

You can almost see the jumbo
video scoreboard overhead
hear the crowd cheer and boo
whilst the two gamesters battle
whether by cards or by dice
for divertissement domination
their fans such serious devotees
they buy branded merchandise
manufactured in sweatshops
they post testimonials or troll
opponents on social media
like bloodthirsty supporters
of ancient chariot racers
these modern zealots affright
when they embrace a favourite
She, all demur smiles in style
as she scores doubled points
He, all gruff and rough exterior
as he attacks her vulnerable blots
but if you think you really know
who is the good gal, the bad guy
examine the two rivals a little
more closely and you discover
that *Sweetness and Light* growls
or hisses under her breath
and *The Hairy Galoot*, well
he applies a lot of conditioner

Tabulae Defixiones

This curse tablet may
Pluto, god of the dead, hear
my clothes, all my clothes
the furtive thief
stole at the baths
for my vindication
everlasting punishment
him condemn

*

Scratched upon lead
these execration letters
call upon the Penates
spirits of my cupboard
to damn the malicious robber
of my salt, my fish
my strawberry jam-pot

*

O Venus, goddess
inflict mendacious Marcus
Marcus who promised love
and lawful union
only to abandon
your dutiful daughter
make sure Marcus suffers
pestilence eternal

*

This my imprecation
made manifest
Proserpina convict
my unworthy, disobedient
slave Candida who
with my silver rings
absconded

*

Dis Pater
great Pluto
the false Roman
Nemmonius Tammonii
porcine imitator
of an equerry
who stole my horses
like the nail I drive
through this malediction
with your sword
his malevolent brain
pierce

*

Sulis Minerva
censure the thief
of my sandals
of Hibernian leather
this summer day
at the public baths
that his feet
blister and bleed

*

Triple Hecate
seek out and punish
the meretricious Volusia
that none others
she infect
that her last taste
before your threshold
a poisonous plant
she ingest

*

Sulis alone and forever
of the Britons
in your sacred name
I cast this curse
on their damnable lead
in their damnable script
against their damnable rule
upon all Romans

*

Neptune, sea god
hear me in the deeps
come forth to execute
your divine wrath
upon inimical raiders
who threaten our lands
infernal Saxones
infernal Saxones
infernal Saxones

*

Upon your profligate priest
P. Flavius Brocchus
O prophetic Apollo
trumpet your rejection
of his immoderate corruption
turning your holy gold
into base, unwatered wine

*

The ignoble general
who sentenced to death
my companions
by decimation
O Mars make his end
sanguinary

*

Fallacious and corrupt
L. Maesius Placidus
tax collector
who oppresses artisans
mighty Hercules
break his bones

*

Sweet, strong Bellona
warrior goddess
my lost, my dead
Antonius vindicate
and all the Selgovae
beyond the wall
eradicate

*

Mercury, god of merchants
damn the timorous traders
who again this short season
lost my cargo of wine amphora
that their immoderate captains
master their business or die

*

Marcus
Marcus
vile Marcus

The Beatles are Fire

With thanks to HazeBruv and all the 'reactioneers'

Maybe one transmission
on black-and-white TV
transformed your whole world
to spectrum colour music
and you no longer lived
in a drab, drab dream
maybe you yearned to be
as old as your sister
so you could slip a ciggy
to the rhythm guitarist
on lunch dates at The Cavern
maybe you cherished, then
passed on your mono copy
of *Rubber Soul*, the one
you played the last track
on the first side, last track
on the first side, last track
on the first side ...
maybe you slogged through
white, white snow from shop
to shop to buy *The BEATLES*
records and pictures and poster
maybe you measured seven years
in your life by their calendar
of album and single releases
maybe you discerned
magical numerology
long before *Number nine*
Number nine in catalogue
entries T 2442, T 2576
and maybe you will always
be a Beatlemaniac

*

And what, other than
the light of genius
shining upon generation
after generation
is the reason now
for screams of joy
tears of sadness
of first-time listeners
who record their reactions
in computer transmissions
who speak to the future

The Beatles are fire
they go crazy

The King of Coif

For Mitchell Lee

When pandemic
prohibitions relaxed
and salons reopened
my usual barber
Rick, you've got
to help me
announced retirement
aged seventy-five
I turned
to an *artiste*
the king of coif
with his tattoos
Doc Martens
ear-lobe plugs
Mitch and I
both masked
he wielded
electric clippers
in a frenzy
of flying hair
like some cat-
and-dog fight
in a loony cartoon
and soon transformed
1970 shagginess
into 2020 shorn
all but my beard
a hands-off zone
by provincial decree
when he said

Come with me

out of the shop
around the corner
down an alley
up against a wall
for a whisker razing
like I was buying
sex or drugs
or both

     *

When later I gazed
at my mirrored face
the remaining beard
was short as my father's
military moustache
and my lips
looked exactly
like his

The Pandora Books

Richard, you lament
we're no longer able
to burn through books
like our younger selves
hungry to devour
every text at speed
but would we trade
the slow savour of words
the knowing of ingredients
from the Italian, the French
the Arabic, the Spanish
how our minds mull
over places and people
so when we read Venice
Prague or Moscow
we hear Venezia
Praha or Moskva
how we speak aloud
Visions d'Anna
ou Le vertige
page after page
carried aloft
never wishing
to come
down

No?

*

Have you heard tell
of the librarian who
began Arturo Belano's
final narration *2666*
and sent word she had
contracted the plague
and how I also started
this tale of murder
murder, murder
and could not breathe
could not stop the pain
could not sleep the sleep
having opened that infectious
book you also started
have you succumbed
to the virus of language
how it mutates
in the presence
of the deadly
printed
word

Yes?

*

We must be careful, Richard
even to catch a glimpse
of light reflected
from a glossy cover
could start a storm
in our eyes, in our brains
and prying apart the boards
of an ancient volume
like the halves of a shell
could change us forever
first you will draw books
with your place marked
by tree roots, then
a codex in flames
in the middle of the air
soon you will detail
pages with written
titles on Painters
Memory, Dream
while I will compose
  \ | /
 — Sun —
  / | \
and in its light
we will open
every book

The Second Time Alice Munro
Asked Me a Question

In the library queue
of babbling inquisitors
she reappeared to ask me
a second quiet question
this time for her husband
who desired to know
whether Jorge Luis Borges'
*A Universal History
of Infamy* comprised
actual bibliographic entries
or secret fabrications
to confound his readers

Off to the lower system
of rectangular rooms
I took her to seek
answers in The N.U.C.
*The National Union Catalog
Pre-1956 Imprints*, where
looking up each author
we discovered entries so near
yet so far from truth
we both felt we were
looking for meaning
in impenetrable dreams

She gave me her phone
number in case any further
information turned up
so later I ascended the stairs
to the seemingly limitless
shelves of books
retrieved Borges' original
Historia universal
de la infamia
and, repeating my quest
in The N.U.C., found
again only fantasies

            *

When she returned
my phone message
she said she and her husband
laughed when I revealed
that he was not alone
that graduate students
of many languages
had posted digital laments
on various internet sites
about Borges' intentions
their voices crying
in the wilderness

Thou

for whom three identical
snowflakes alight upon
an upturned face

for whom imaginal dragonflies
wrinkle-winged and damp
emerge into the air

for whom waterfall run-off
roars over rock
in foam crescendo

for whom glaciers
roll granite debris
with abandon

for whom ancient ice
releases ancient oxygen
to ring a drinking-glass

for whom the grape
gives up nectar
and a beautiful stain

for whom Grass Pink
Rose Pogonia and Calypso
orchids lure eye-glance

for whom tears well up
and slip down
from sorrow and joy

for whom the heart drum
beats the rhythm
of all dance

Three Bird Hokku

Longship of ravens
sails upon northerly wind
O the din, the din

Around the statue
of crouching, weeping Buddha
a hermit thrush feeds

Cardinal blushes
from crest to tail on a branch
where two squirrels mate

To Keep Now Still

Working title of William Golding's *The Scorpion God*

The boy-king is dead
from fracture and malaria
long dead the kings of Egypt
all their gold and alabaster
will not call them forth
again to the Black Land
their chipped, eyeless statues
feign eternity, a still
point that never exists
outside a starry life
wheeling, flowing, burning
leaving Great House behind
on display in glass cases
we create to keep *now* forever
when every Pharaoh, everyone
will become as mummy dust
and even the pyramids
over time will be levelled
and gone

Tutankhamun's Mask

The mask that encased the boy-king's face
looms before my face in its museum case
as I dare to imagine wearing the relic
the mask of the golden breath of dawn
carnelian and turquoise coming forth by day
azure stone the sky at Nilotic twilight
can anyone hear me through burnished gold
my lips desert dry, papyrus dry my skin
my arms cross with the crook and the flail
although I have not conspired with demons
the cobra and the vulture upon my brow
fail to protect me from the kiss of chaos
my blessèd brain through the nostrils gone
lungs, liver, intestines, stomach reside in jars
priests remove, erect, replace the royal member
sacred salts of natron infuse the earthly body
the ka strains beneath linen, gold, wood, stone
to recognize the visage of father the sun
but sees only a reflection in the tempered glass
my eyes overlaying the empty gaze of Pharaoh

Tysca, Our Bird

Hearken

he never takes to gloved fist
swears an oath only
to nest-mate and fledglings
he seeks, he hunts the kill
with sharp neb, sharp claws
British hare, mouse, snake
or the already dead
he rends bloody flesh
feeds on red tearings
cleans full-grown feathers
wing and tail atop
ashen bough or oaken limb
always ready to fly and swoop
hear his call, high scream
above dales, over both
the lord's son
clothed in wool
and the swain's son
swathed in hides
he sings our fearsome song
we Saxons who hold
these seaboard lands
who speak our word-lore
free as *Tysca*

this hawk

Word Temple

O
we
build
a temple
from the sky
down to ground
recitation and inscription
laminate in words by ideograms in jewel
we call up
exotic timbers
for the holy shrine
sweet pine of stories
strong oak of ancestor hills
fragrant sandalwood of far families
carried to us on the currents of five rivers
laminate in words by memories in lacquer by ideograms in jewel
we request
the ore of metals
copper from mute canyon
tin from silent mountain peak
drawn upon roads by ox-driven carts
ore crushed and heated and smelted and blended
alloy poured and cast and cooled to hymns and prayers
laminate in words by singing bells in bronze by ideograms in jewel
I am the writer and you are the reader
you are the teller and I am the listener
I am the chant and you are the chanter
you are the priest and I am the acolyte
I am the teller and you are the listener
you are the chant and I am the chanter
I am the priest and you are the acolyte
you are the writer and I am the reader

Acknowledgements

"Golden Joining, Golden Repair" first appeared online in *True Identity: An Anthology of Writing, Poetry and Photography*, edited by April Bulmer, from Hidden Brook Press (2021).

"Off Two Decks" first appeared in F*orest City Open Mic Poetry at the Mykonos: Season Anthology 2019-2020*, edited by Robyn Marie Butt (2020).

"Pyramidion" first appeared in *The Beauty of Being Elsewhere: Poems of Journey and Sojourn*, edited by John B. Lee, from Hidden Brook Press (2021).

"Revs" first appeared in *Window Fishing: The Night We Caught Beatlemania*, edited by John B. Lee, from Hidden Brook Press (2014).

"Silverpoint" first appeared online on Richard A. Kirk's BlogSpot (2006).

"The King of Coif" first appeared online in *Dénouement: A Poetry Anthology*, edited by Andreas Gripp, from Beliveau Books (2021).

"The Second Time Alice Munro Asked Me a Question" first appeared online in *Framed & Familiar, 101 Portraits: An International Anthology of Poetry and Photography*, edited by Antony Di Nardo, from SandCrab Books (2022).

My thanks to Don Gutteridge, to the publisher, Tai Grove, at Wet Ink Books, to Richard A. Kirk for the cover art, and to the editors listed above.

My especial thanks to the poets of the group in London, Ontario.

John Tyndall lives in London, Ontario with an Angora tuxedo cat named Buddy. His recent books include *Listen to People* (Hidden Brook, 2020) and *The Fee for Exaltation* (Black Moss, 2007). His poems have also appeared in many print and online anthologies, such as *Translating Horses: The Line, The Thread, The Underside* (Baseline, 2015), edited by Jessica Hiemstra and Gillian Sze, and the journals *The Windsor Review* and *Devour: Art & Lit Canada*.

www.ingramcontent.com/pod-product-compliance
Lightning Source LLC
Chambersburg PA
CBHW031244120626
46545CB00007B/2635